Adobe Prem

to Advance Guide

A Comprehensive Step-by-Step Guide for
novice and Expert to Master Video Editing,
Graphic effects, and Hidden Features for
Cinematic Excellence.

By

David G. Green

Table of Content

Introduction

There is no doubt that Adobe Premiere Pro is the leading video editing software that is used by the elites in the video editing world. So, if you are reading this guide, congratulations, you are about to step into a world of video editing that you didn't even know existed. Whether you want advanced effects or simple color grading, this ebook caters to you. We will be walking you through step-by-step tutorials and drop tips and tricks on the way. Learn how to create captivating videos, polish your footage with seamless transitions, and unleash your creativity with the powerful tools and features offered by Adobe Premiere Pro.

GETTING STARTED

In this part of the ebook, we will show you the basic things you need to learn about Adobe Premiere Pro. Some of them include starting up your software and optimizing its performance.

Prerequisites

To use Adobe Premiere Pro, you need to have basic video editing concepts. You must also be comfortable using a computer because you will use a laptop. A lot. Also, you should be familiar with concepts such as clipping, timeline, transitions, and cuts.

Installing Premiere Pro

If you don't have Adobe Premiere Pro on your computer, you must install it. Follow the steps below

Step 1

You can purchase Adobe Premiere Pro from the official website. After the purchase, you will get a license to access the software.

Step 2

Go to the website and sign in to your Adobe account. Go to the "downloads" section and locate the Adobe Premiere Pro installer.

Step 3

Once the download is complete, locate the installer file on your computer

Step 4

You will be guided through the installation process by the installer.

Step 5

You will be prompted to sign in with your Adobe ID or Creative Cloud account. Enter your credentials to authenticate your license or subscription.

Step 6

Wait for the installation process to be completed before launching the application.

Optimizing performance

To effectively use Adobe Premiere Pro, it needs to be optimized. Optimizing also ensures smooth editing.

- The first thing is to ensure that you use a powerful computer. The system's RAM should be 16GB or more, and the system should have dedicated video ram.
- Always keep your Adobe Premiere Pro Software updated. Regularly check for updates so that bugs in your software can be fixed.
- When starting a new project, ensure the settings match your video's

specifications. Use the appropriate frame rate, resolution, and other settings to avoid unnecessary processing overhead.

There are other ways to optimize your Adobe Premiere Pro, but the ones above are some of the essential ones.

Adobe Authorized Training Centers

Adobe Authorized Training Centers are educational centers that Adobe authorizes. These centers meet specific requirements set by Adobe to ensure high-quality training experiences for individuals seeking to learn and enhance their skills in Adobe software. These Centers offer a wide range of courses, and they are designed to cater to different skill levels.

Chapter 1: TOURING ADOBE PREMIERE PRO

In this chapter, we will briefly tour Adobe Premiere Pro. You will learn how to create your first edits and be informed about Keyboard shortcuts. We will be your tour guide. Follow us.

Performing Nonlinear Editing in Premiere Pro

Performing nonlinear editing in Adobe Premiere Pro means working with multiple video and audio tracks simultaneously, making nondestructive edits, and arranging clips on a timeline.

Step 1

Import your media into Premiere Pro.

Step 2

Next, create a new sequence. Go to File > New > Sequence.

Step 3

Go to the timeline panel, then drag and drop your media file into different tracks.

Step 4

Next, use the Razor Tool (C) to cut clips at specific points on the timeline.

Step 5

Now you will need to add transitions. To add transitions between clips, position the play head at the desired location. Go to the Effects panel, and search for the desired transition effects.

Step 6

Use the Program Monitor to preview your edits in real-time. Finally, go to File > Export > Media to export your project.

Expanding the workflow

This involves incorporating additional features, tools, and techniques to enhance your editing process and achieve more professional results. Different advanced techniques help refine your edits. Some of the advanced techniques include using keyboard shortcuts and utilizing the trim mode for precise trimming.

Touring the Premiere Pro interface

If this software is going to be of any benefit to you, we must take you on a quick tour of Adobe Premiere Pro. Here are some of the main components of Adobe Premiere Pro.

- **Toolbar**

This is positioned below the menu bar. It contains tools for trimming, editing, working with text, etc.

- **Menu Bar**

The menu bar is located at the top of the application window and provides access to various menus for file management, editing, effects, and more.

- **Source Monitor**

The Source Monitor is handy for previewing and selecting your imported media files before placing them on the timeline.

Hands-on: Edit Your First Video

Now that you know the basics of Adobe Premiere Pro, it is time for you to try your hands on editing a video. Are you excited? Let's do it.

Step 1

Go to File > Import or use the Media Browser panel to locate and import your files.

Step 2

Next, Right-click in the Project panel and select "New Item" > "Sequence" to create a new sequence.

Step 3

Organize your assets by creating bins or folders. To keep your files organized, drag and drop them in the appropriate bins.

Step 4

In the Project panel, please select the desired clips and drag them to the Timeline panel. You can use the Ripple Edit Tool to trim clips without leaving gaps.

Step 5

To make precise edits, use your razor tool.

Step 6

Next, go to the Effects panel, search for the desired transition effect, and drag it to the edit point between two clips on the timeline.

Step 7

Go to the Effects panel, choose the desired effect, and drag it onto a clip on the timeline. Use the Audio Track Mixer panel to adjust audio levels, apply effects, and mix your audio tracks.

Step 8

Remember to use the program monitor to preview and fine-tune your edit.

Step 9

Once satisfied with your edits, go to File > Export > Media to export your video.

Using and setting keyboard shortcuts

Premiere Pro provides flexibility to customize and assign keyboard shortcuts according to your preferences. To access your keyboard shortcuts, go to Edit > Keyboard Shortcuts.

Keep in mind that Premiere Pro has a set of default keyboard shortcuts. These shortcuts are designed to provide efficient access to commonly used functions.

To use a default shortcut, locate the desired command or function in the Keyboard

Shortcuts dialog box and note the assigned shortcut key(s) on the right.

Chapter 2: Setting Up a Project

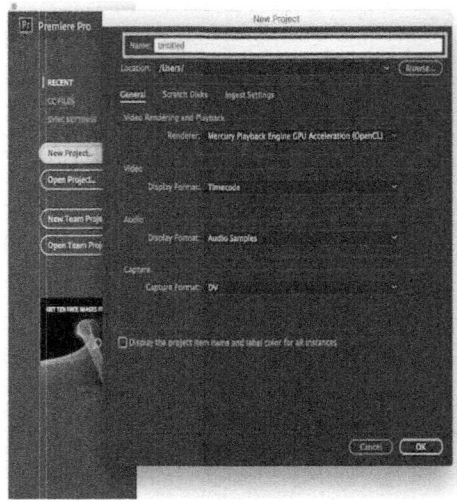

Now that we have taken a tour of Adobe Premiere Pro, it is time for us to show you how you can set up a project in Adobe Premiere Pro. In this chapter, you will see how you can create a project and explore the project settings

Creating a Project

Here is how you can create a project in Adobe Premiere Pro.

Step 1

Launch Adobe Premiere Pro.

Step 2

Click on "New Project" to start a new project.

Step 3

Choose a name for your project and type it in the dialog box.

Step 4

In the New Project dialog box, you can specify the location of the project's scratch disks

Step 5

In the New Project dialog box, you can specify the settings for your sequence. Remember, choose a preset that matches most of your footage's specifications.

Step 6

Choose a workspace layout that best suits your editing style and preferences. Finally, click "OK": After providing the necessary project details and settings, click the "OK" button to create the project.

Setting Up a Sequence

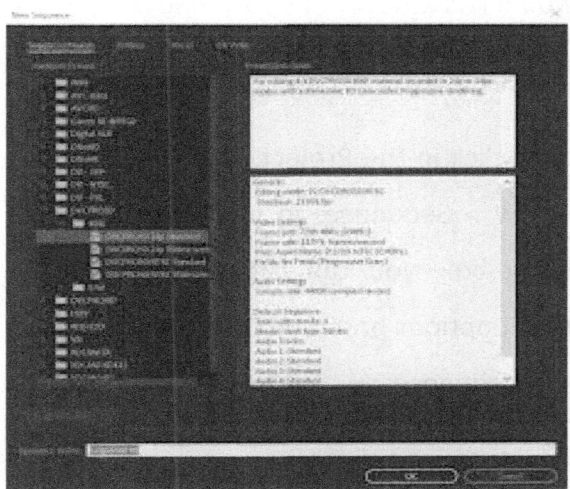

Setting you a sequence is much like setting up a project, except with a few differences. Follow the steps below.

Step 1

Launch your Adobe Premiere Pro.

Step 2

Next, import your media. By now, you should know how to import media.

Step 3

Right-click in the Project panel or go to File > New > Sequence. In the New Sequence dialog box, you can choose from various preset options based on the intended use of your sequence.

Step 4

If you wish to customize the settings, select "Settings" in the New Sequence dialog box.

Step 5

Go to the New Sequence dialog box, and choose the preview file format. So that you know, the preview files help improve playback performance while editing. The default option, "I-Frame Only MPEG," is recommended for most projects.

Step 6

Now you need to enter a name for your sequence and choose a location to save it within your project.

Step 7

Look at the summary of your sequence settings in the New Sequence dialog box. Make sure they match your requirements. Make any necessary adjustments before clicking the "OK" button.

Explore the Project Settings

What is the point of the project settings in Adobe Premiere Pro? It is simple. The Project Settings allow you to customize various parameters and preferences for your project. Here is how to explore the project settings.

Step 1

Go to File > Project Settings > General.

Step 2

Modify the project name in the General tab and the scratch disk settings. The scratch disks define the location where Premiere Pro stores temporary files during the editing process.

Step 3

Remember that If you're working with tape-based media and intend to capture footage directly into Premiere Pro, you can modify the Capture Settings in the General Project Settings dialog box.

Step 4

The Scratch Disks tab in the Project Settings dialog box helps specify the location and organization of the temporary files generated during the editing process.

Step 5

In the video rendering and playback tab, you can adjust settings related to rendering and playback performance.

Other features of the project settings that you can explore include:

- Audio settings
- Label settings
- Markers settings
- Video rendering and playback settings

Chapter 3: IMPORTING MEDIA

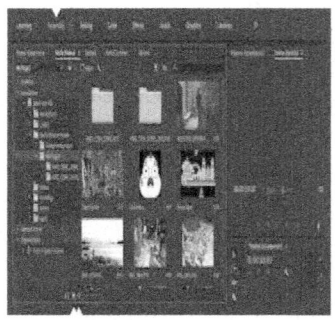

If you've gotten this far, you know the importance of Importing media files before you can carry out any project in Adobe Premiere Pro. Let us begin by seeing how to import media files into your Adobe Premiere Pro workspace.

Starting The Lesson Importing Media Files

You are about to start a project in Adobe Premiere Pro, and you are lost on how to import the media files that you need. Don't fret; follow the steps below.

Step 1

Launch Adobe Premiere Pro.

Step 2

If you're starting a new project, go to File > New > Project and follow the prompts to create a new project. If you already have a project, open it by going to File > Open Project.

Step 3

Navigate to Window > Media Browser to open the Media Browser panel.

Step 4

In the Media Browser panel, navigate to the folder or directory where your media files are stored. Find your desired file by navigating through your system files.

Step 5

In the Media Browser panel, you can preview media files by clicking on them

Step 6

Click on the media files you want to import into your project.

Working With Ingest Options and Proxy Media Working with The Media Browser Panel

There are several methods provided by Adobe Premiere Pro which allow ingesting of media and working with proxy files. Ingesting media refers to the process of importing media files into your Premiere Pro project

Step 1

Start by creating a new project.

Step 2

Next, proceed to the Window menu and select Media Browser to open the Media Browser panel.

Step 3

Go to the folder in the Media Browser and select where your media files are located.

Step 4

When you have seen the files that you want to import, there are two options you have: direct import or ingest.

Step 5

Go to the Ingest Settings dialog box, and choose your preferred options. Options include Copy, create proxies, Transcode, and Handle length. After you've chosen your desired options, select OK to start the Ingest process.

Step 6

Next, Adobe Premiere Pro will begin to start copying and transcoding the media files based on the settings that you selected.

Step 7

Now that the Ingest process is complete, the imported and proxy files will appear in the project panel.

Importing Still Image Files

If you wish to work with still image files in Adobe Premiere Pro, here is how you can do it.

Step 1

Start by creating a new project or using an existing one.

Step 2

Go to the project panel, right-click in the space, and select "Import" from the context menu.

Step 3

Go to the import dialog and go to the folder where the still images you want to import are.

Step 4

Click the import button. The imported still images will show up in the project panel.

Using Adobe Stock

When you use Adobe Stock, you get access to royalty-free stock assets, which include images and videos that can be licensed and used in different projects.

Step 1

Open Adobe Premiere Pro and navigate to the "Essential Graphics" panel or the "Project" panel.

Step 2

Go to the search bar, and look for the video or motion graphics.

Step 3

Go through the results of the search. Click on an asset so that you can preview it.

Step 4

If you find an asset you'd like to use, click on the "License" button.

Step 5

Once you've licensed the asset, it will be available for download. Click on "download."

Step 6

Go to the "Project" panel and click the "Import" button to import the downloaded asset.

Step 7

Drag and drop the imported asset to use it in your project.

Recording a Voice-over

You can record a voice-over directly from Adobe Premiere Pro, thanks to various tools provided by the software. Let's see how to do a voice-over using Adobe Premiere Pro quickly.

Step 1

Set up your recording equipment.

Step 2

Open your Adobe Premiere Pro and go ahead to create a new project.

Step 3

Go to your timeline and set the playhead to the starting point of your voice-over.

Step 4

Ensure the audio track where you want to record your voice-over is enabled. Next, allow recording mode by going to the "window" menu and choosing "Audio track mixer."

Step 5

In the Audio Track Mixer panel, select the appropriate microphone as the input source for the voice-over recording.

Step 6

In the audio track controls, click the "R" button to arm the track.

Step 7

Start recording.

Customizing The Media Cache

Media Cache is used in Adobe Premiere Pro to access temporary files for better and smoother playback. The following steps will show you how to customize the media cache.

Step 1

Launch Adobe Premiere Pro.

Step 2

Proceed to the "Edit" menu and choose "Preferences."

Step 3

Click on the "Media cache" tab in the preferences dialog box.

Step 4

To change the location, click the "Browse" button next to the "Location" field, and select a different folder or drive where you want to store the Media Cache files.

Step 5

You can adjust the "maximum disk cache size," which will determine the maximum amount of disk space that the media cache can use.

Chapter 4: ORGANIZING MEDIA

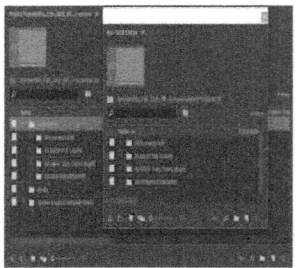

For efficient video editing, organizing media in Adobe Premiere Pro is vital. If your media is appropriately organized, you can quickly locate and manage your files. In this chapter, we will examine some critical aspects of media organization.

Using The Project Panel

The project panel is a central hub where media assets and sequences are managed. It allows you to import, preview and organize your media assets. This panel can be found in the lower-left corner of the interface.

If you wish to import media into the panel, use the regular file import method or the "Media Browser" panel.

When the media files are imported, they can be organized within the project panel. Right-click within the panel and choose "New Bin" to create a new folder-like container. You can also create nested bins to categorize further and organize your assets. Drag and drop media files into the desired bins to manage them accordingly.

Working with Bins

Bins act as containers within the project panel, aiding you to categorize and group related items together. To create a bin, follow these steps.

Step 1

Open the project panel.

Step 2

Select "New Bin" and right-click within the project panel. This will create a new bin.

Step 3

To create nested bins, right-click on an existing bin and select "New Bin" again. A sub-bin within the parent bin will be created. You can nest multiple levels of bins to organize your assets further.

Reviewing footage

To preview media files, double-click on a clip within the Project Panel or use the Source Monitor. Double-clicking a clip opens it in the Source Monitor, where you can play, scrub, and review the clip. This allows you to assess the content and make selections before adding it to your timeline.

Freeform View

You can find the freeform view at the bottom of the project panel. The size of your clips can be adjusted using the slider next to the freeform view button. The freeform view also allows you to organize your clips without using a grid. It will let you lay out your clips from top to bottom or left to right.

Modifying clips

Modifying your clips in Adobe Premiere Pro helps you to achieve your desired results. For example, you may want to trim and cut a clip to fit your timeline. To trim and cut a clip, select the clip in the timeline and position the play head to the desired position. Use your razor tool and cut the playhead position. Remove the wanted clip by selecting it and pressing "Delete."

Chapter 5: MASTERING THE ESSENTIALS OF VIDEO EDITING

Welcome to the fifth chapter of your journey. Here we will show you some basic things you must know to become an excellent video editor. If you are good at editing videos using Adobe Premiere Pro, don't blink while reading this chapter. Just kidding (Am I?)

Starting the Lesson

Some of the critical aspects of video editing in Premiere Pro you should keep in mind include, Importing and organizing footage, timeline and sequencing, audio editing, etc. In this lesson, we will look at some of them.

Using the Source Monitor

The source monitor is a great tool that lets users preview their media assets before adding them to the timeline. To use this powerful tool, follow the steps below.

Step 1

Open your project in Adobe Premiere Pro. The Source Monitor is located in the top-left corner of the interface.

Step 2

Go to the project panel and locate the clip you want to preview and edit. Next, drag it and drop it on the source monitor.

Step 3

The Source Monitor provides standard playback controls to preview your clip. You can use the play button, scrub through the clip, or use keyboard shortcuts such as Spacebar to play/pause, JKL keys for playback control, and L and J keys for fast forward and rewind.

Step 4

Using the Source Monitor, you can modify a clip's playback speed for quick slow-motion or fast-motion effects. Right-click on the clip in the Source Monitor, select "Speed/Duration," and adjust the speed percentage as desired.

Navigating the Timeline panel

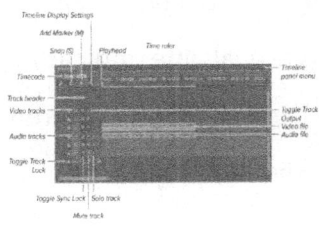

The Timeline panel is where you assemble and arrange your video and audio clips to create your final sequence in Adobe Premiere Pro. This panel gives you a comprehensive view of your project's timeline, allowing you to navigate, edit, and manipulate your clips.

To navigate the Timeline panel, you must know how to open it. The Timeline panel is located in the lower part of the interface. If you can't see it, go to the "Window" menu and select "Timeline" to open it. You must also know how to move the play head to navigate the timeline effectively. To move the play head (the vertical line indicating the current position), click on the desired location on the ruler above the timeline.

Using essential editing commands

Here are some basic editing commands you want to remember when working with Adobe Premiere Pro.

● Play/Pause

Press the spacebar to play or pause your video in the Timeline or Program Monitor. You can also use the L key to play the video forward at different speeds and the J key backward.

● Ripple Delete

Choose a clip in the Timeline and press the Delete key to remove it. It is important to note that Premiere Pro automatically closes the gap created by the deleted clip, ensuring that the rest of the timeline remains intact.

- Copy and Paste

To duplicate a clip or a group of clips, select them and press Ctrl+C (Command+C on Mac) to copy. Move the play head to the desired position and press Ctrl+V (Command+V on Mac) to paste the copied clips into the timeline.

Performing storyboard-style editing

This means Organizing your video clips and visual elements into a sequence that looks like a storyboard. This approach is perfect if you are looking to plan and structure your video before going into the finer details.

Step 1

Import all of your video clips into the project panel.

Step 2

Go ahead to create a new sequence. To do this, Right-click in the Project panel, select "New Item," and choose "Sequence.

Step 3

In the Project panel, create a new bin specifically for your storyboard elements.

Step 4

Next, drag the storyboard elements from the bin onto the Timeline in the order you want them to appear. Each element should represent a specific scene or shot in your video.

Step 5

Use the Selection Tool to select and trim the duration of each storyboard element on the Timeline.

Step 6

You can add any audio tracks that you deem necessary. Finally, review and refine.

Chapter 6: WORKING WITH CLIPS AND MARKERS

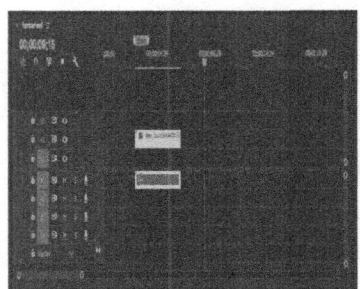

Working with clips and markers helps you to organize and manage your footage effectively. This part of this book will explore all you need to know about using these clips to make video editing much easier. Beyond using these clips, we will also show you how to move them.

Starting the Lesson

Markers show essential points and aid you in positioning and arranging your clips.

Markers also come in handy when you wish to identify an action or sound. There are several types of markers, and they are:

- Comment
- Chapter
- Segmentation marker
- Web link

Using the Program Monitor Controls

The program monitor controls are essential, playing back individual clips in the source monitor. To use this feature, you must prepare the clips you want to add to a sequence and then set your in and out points. After setting your points, you need to specify the source of the clip.

The program monitor is responsible for playing back the sequence of the clips that are being assembled. It also gives you a view of the active sequence in a timeline panel. Using the Program Monitor, you can sequence markers and specify sequence In and Out points. Where frames are added or excluded are the points In and Out.

Setting the Playback Resolution

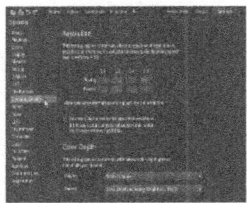

If you wish to optimize performance, you can use quality settings for your image when playback is paused or active.

Step 1

Start by clicking the settings menu. The settings menu is on the upper right corner of the screen.

Step 2

Choose a lower resolution, like 1:2.

Playing Back VR Video

You may have caught an excellent video on camera, and you want a particular section of the video to be played on a loop. If that is the case, follow the simple steps below.

Step 1

Start by opening your Adobe Premiere Pro Software

Step 2

Look for a plus icon on the project panel and select the playback.

Step 3

Left click, hold, drag, and drop. Click OK.

Step 4

Now click on the playback loop.

Using Markers

As we mentioned earlier, markers are tabs that allow you to identify essential parts of the video. Ever used sticky notes? Think of markers ad sticky notes, except that they are for videos.

Part of using markers in Adobe Premiere Pro includes knowing how to add them. To add a marker, tap the M key on your keyboard, and you will find a new marker at the playhead. The markers panel can be located along with Effects and Metadata.

Using Sync Locks and Track Locks

When editing a video, you may want one of the tracks not to move in sync with the rest. This can be achieved using Sync and Track Locks.

Step 1

To use a Sync lock, open your project.

Step 2

Right-click on the gaps between clips on the first video track. Next, choose Ripple Delete.

Step 3

Now press on control Z to undo the Ripple Delete. Go ahead to switch the toggle sync lock icon off.

Step 4

Now right-click the gap between clips on the first video track. Choose "Ripple Delete." Undo the Ripple Delete.

Step 5

Choose the Ripple tool. Grab the right edge of the first clip in the video track 1. Go ahead to drag about an inch to the left.

Step 6

In like manner, grab the right edge of the first clip in the video track 4. Also, drag it to the left.

To use Track Lock, follow the steps below.

Step 1

Start by ensuring that all the tracks have Toggle sync lock on.

Step 2

In video track 4, click the track lock icon.

Step 3

Attempt to do a Ripple Delete and see if the locked track is unaffected.

Working with Gaps in The sequence

To manipulate gaps effectively, there are a few techniques and features you can use. Let's explore a few of them in the next paragraph.

To insert a gap, first, create a gap in your sequence. Next, position the play head at the desired location where you want to insert the gap. Go ahead to Press the "Delete" key on your keyboard. This action removes the selected clips and creates a gap in their place.

If you wish to have a gap between two clips, select the gap by clicking on it. Next, right-click and choose "Ripple Delete" from the context menu.

Selecting Clips

You can select your clips in multiple ways when using Adobe Premiere Pro. We will show you one or two ways to achieve it.

Step 1

This is the **Click Selection** method. Start by moving your cursor to the Program Monitor or Timeline panel.

Step 2

Go ahead to position the cursor over the clip that you want to select.

Step 3

Select the clip by clicking on it.

Let us also look at the **Lasso Method**

Step 1

Position your cursor in an empty area of the Timeline panel.

Step 2

To draw a Lasso, click and drag the cursor.

Step 3

The mouse button should be released to select the clips within the Lasso.

Moving Clips

You can move clips within your sequence to adjust or rearrange their position using Adobe Premiere Pro. Follow these steps.

Step 1

Select the clip(s) you want to move by clicking on them.

Step 2

Ensure that the selection tool is active.

Step 3

Click on the clips in the timeline panel. Make sure the clips are selected.

Step 4

Next, drag the clip(s) to the desired new position within the sequence.

Extracting and Deleting Segments

Extracting and deleting segments helps remove created content or create new edits.

Step 1

Select the clip(s) in the Timeline panel to identify the segment you want to extract or delete

Step 2

Use the shortcut C to choose the razor tool. Employ the Selection tool to select the segment you want to extract or delete.

Step 3

Once you've selected the segment, press the "Delete" key on your keyboard to extract it from the sequence.

Chapter 7: ADDING TRANSITIONS

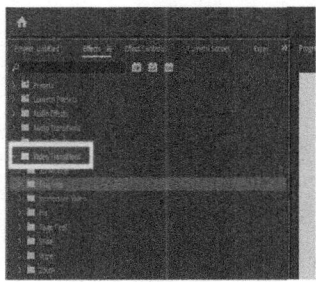

To create smooth and visually appealing transitions from one shot to another, it is essential to know how to add transitions. One of the importance of transitions is that they help to continuity and flow of your video.

Starting The Lesson

In this lesson, we will understand transition effects and why you should use them in your projects. Even more importantly, we will explore how to use them effectively in your shots. Read on.

What are Transition Effects?

These are effects that are added by Premiere Pro that can be added at the beginning or end of a clip. It can be used to create a fade in or fade out or a gradual shift from one scene to another.

Transitions add creators to change between clips seamlessly. If your video has too many cuts, you will be thankful for transition effects.

The Importance of Clip Handles

Clip handles are the extra footage available at the beginning and end of a video clip beyond what is used in the final edited sequence. Clip handles are great for seamless and smooth transitions between clips. Having clip handles allows you to extend the duration of a clip without cutting off any content, ensuring a polished and professional-looking transition.

Regarding reframing and positioning, clip handles offer a lot of flexibility. By having additional footage at the beginning and end of a clip, you can adjust the position, scale, or rotation without revealing any empty spaces or sudden cuts.

Adding Video Transition Effects

Adding a video transition effect isn't as daunting as it sounds if you follow the proper steps. Allow us to show you how to get it done in a few steps.

Step 1

Open your project. Search for the clips you want to edit and click "Open."

Step 2

Create a new sequence from the clip by selecting the project panel.

Step 3

Scroll down and select Windows in the menu bar. Next, scroll down and click on **Effects** if there is no checkmark. You will see the effects tab in the project panel. Clicking on it will give you access to all the effects in Adobe Premiere Pro.

Step 4

Go to the Effects panel and navigate to video transitions. Now, expand the categories and choose the one you like. To apply the transitions to your timeline, drag the desired transition and drop it at the beginning or end of the clip.

Using A/B Mode to Fine-tune a Transition

Here is how you can fine-tune a transition using A/B mode in Adobe Premiere Pro.

Step 1

Load your project after you have opened Premiere Pro.

Step 2

On the timeline, place the clips that you want to make transitions between. There should also be a slight overlap where the transition will happen.

Step 3

Select the transition area by clicking and dragging over the overlapping section between the two clips.

Step 4

Go to the Effects panel, and search for the desired transition effect. Drag and drop the transition effect onto the selected transition area on the timeline.

Step 5

With the transition selected on the timeline, go to the Effect Controls panel. You should see the parameters for the transition effect.

Step 6

Look for the A/B mode option in the Effect Controls panel. It should be a toggle button labeled "A/B.

Step 7

Toggle the A/B mode on. This will split the transition area into two halves: A and B.

Step 8

You can now adjust the parameters of the transition effect separately for the A and B sides. Play the timeline to preview the transition and make further adjustments. Once satisfied with the transition, you can toggle off the A/B mode.

Adding Audio Transition effects

Adding an audio transition involves similar steps to Adding a video transition. Because we want you to be good at using Adobe

75

Premiere Pro, we will show you how to add audio transitions.

Step 1

Open your project. Search for the clips you want to edit and click "Open."

Step 2

Create a new sequence from the clip by selecting the project panel.

Step 3

Scroll down and select Windows in the menu bar. Next, scroll down and click on Effects if there is no checkmark. You will see the effects tab in the project panel. Clicking on it will give you access to all the effects in Adobe Premiere Pro.

Step 4

Go to the Effects panel and navigate to audio transitions. Now, expand the categories and choose the one you like. To apply the transitions to your timeline, drag the desired transition and drop it at the beginning or end of the clip.

Chapter 8: MASTERING ADVANCED EDITING TECHNIQUES

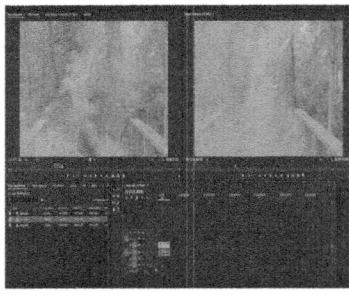

If you have read up to this point, we know you are now ready to explore advanced editing techniques in Adobe Premiere Pro. Relax; it isn't as complicated as it appears. All you need to do is follow the steps carefully, and you'd be good to go.

Starting The Lesson

In this chapter, we will start the lesson by performing a four-point edit. A four-point edit is a technique used in video editing to precisely place a clip or segment into a timeline based on four edit points: the in and out points of the source clip and the in and out points of the destination timeline. Let's delve deeper.

Performing a Four-point Edit

A four-point edit allows for precise control over placement and clip duration. Follow these steps to perform a four-point edit.

Step 1

Start by Importing the source clip.

Step 2

In the Project panel, locate the source clip and double-click on it to open it in the Source Monitor. Play through the clip and find the desired in and out points for the segment you want to edit into your timeline

Step 3

Navigate to your timeline where you want to place the clip. Also, play through the timeline and find the desired in and out points for the segment where you want to insert the clip.

Step 4

Now it is time to perform a four-point edit. Drag and drop - In the Source Monitor, click and drag the selected portion of the source clip to the timeline. Position the play head in the timeline where you want the edit to begin and drop the clip. Premiere Pro will automatically perform a four-point edit based on the in and out points of both the source clip and the timeline.

Changing Clip Playback Speed

If the playback speed of your video is too fast, there is always the option of slowing it down. Here is how you can do it.

Step 1

Start by importing the clip you want to adjust the playback speed for into your Premiere Pro project

Step 2

Ensure that the settings match the settings of your clip before changing the playback speed.

Step 3

Now, locate the clip in your Project panel and drag it onto the timeline to add it to your sequence.

Step 4

With the clip selected on the timeline, go to the "Effects Control" panel.

Step 5

Enable time remapping to change the playback speed of the clip. A stopwatch icon is next to the "Time remapping," which can be used to create keyframes.

Step 6

Now that the keyframes are created, the speed of the clip can now be adjusted. Move the play head in the timeline to where you want the speed change to begin.

Then, in the "Effects Control" panel, find the line representing the keyframes and click on it. Drag the line up or down to increase or decrease the speed, respectively.

Replacing Clips and Media

The "replace footage" feature allows you to swap out a clip or media file without affecting any effects.

Step 1

Identify the clip you want to replace.

Step 2

Import the new clip or media file that you want to use as a replacement into your Premiere Pro project.

Step 3

Select the clip that you want to replace in your timeline.

Step 4

"Replace Footage": Right-click on the selected clip, and from the context menu, choose "Replace Footage" and then select "File..." or "Clip...". This will open a file selection window

Step 5

Go to the file selection window and navigate to the replacement clip location. Click "OK" to confirm

Nesting sequences

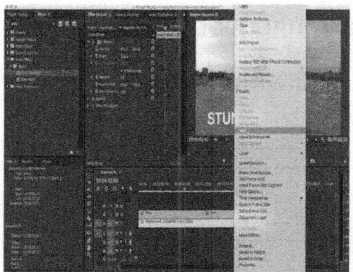

This technique can group multiple clips and effects into a single nested sequence.

Step 1

Go to File > New > Sequence to create a new nested sequence.

Step 2

Import the clips you want to include in your nested sequence into your project. Ensure you arrange the clips in the order you want them to appear.

Step 3

With your clips arranged on the timeline, select all the clips you want to include in the nested sequence.

Step 4

Choose "Nest" after right-clicking on the selected clips. Set a name for the nested sequence: In the dialog box that appears, you can set a name for the nested sequence.

Step 5

After creating the nested sequence, you can double-click on it in the project panel to open it in a new timeline.

Step 6

After you've finished editing the nested sequence, close the nested sequence timeline and return to your main timeline.

Performing Regular Trimming

Performing regular trimming in Adobe Premiere Pro involves adjusting the in and out points of a clip to change its duration or remove unwanted portions.

Step 1

Import the clip you want to edit into your Premiere Pro project.

Step 2

Next, drag the clip from the Project panel and drop it onto the timeline to add it to your sequence.

Step 3

Click on the clip in the timeline to select it.

Step 4

You can use the Trim monitor to do regular trimming. Go to Window > Trim Monitor to open the Trim Monitor panel.

Step 5

In the Trim Monitor panel, you can choose the trim mode that suits your needs. Once satisfied with the trim adjustment, click the "Apply" button on the Trim Monitor.

Performing Advanced Trimming

Advanced trimming involves using more precise trimming techniques than regular trimming can offer.

Step 1

Choose the Ripple Edit Tool at the top of the timeline.

Step 2

Right-click on the clip you want to trim and select "Trim Edit" from the context menu.

Step 3

Now, hover your cursor over the edge of the clip in the timeline until you see a bracket icon. Click and drag the bracket to trim the clip inwards or outwards.

Step 4

Pressing Alt/Option and clicking on the edge of a clip will perform a ripple trim in that direction without affecting adjacent clips.

Step 5

While the sequence plays, pressing the J key will play the clip in reverse, the L key will play it forward, and the K key will pause playback.

Step 6

Go to Window > Trim Monitor. In the Trim Monitor, you can see both the outgoing and incoming frames of the trim. You can use the arrow keys on your keyboard to nudge the trim points frame by frame.

Chapter 9: PUTTING CLIPS IN MOTION

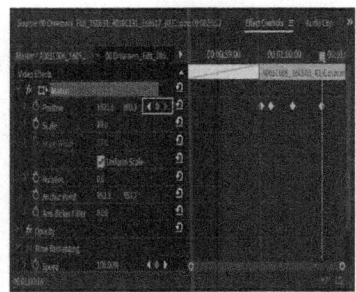

Putting your clip into motion can be done using animation and motion effects. This means that you can create dynamic and visually engaging videos.

Starting The Lesson

In this lesson, we will see how you can adjust the motion effect to get the best results for your videos. Did you know that the position of your clip can also be changed? All these and more will be unveiled as we dig into this chapter.

Adjusting the Motion Effect

Adjusting the Motion effect in Adobe Premiere Pro allows you to fine-tune the position, scale, rotation, and opacity of a clip.

Step 1

As always, import your clip into Adobe Premiere Pro.

Step 2

Add the clip to the timeline.

Step 3

In the Effects Control panel, locate the Motion effect for the selected clip.

Step 4

To change the position of the clip, modify the values for the Position property. You can do this by clicking and dragging the clip directly in the Program Monitor or entering numerical values in the Effects Control panel.

Step 5

If you wish to resize the clip, modify the values for the Scale property. Changing the scale affects both the width and height of the clip.

Step 6

Modifying the value for the Rotation property. Positive values rotate the clip clockwise, while negative values rotate it counterclockwise.

Working With Keyframe Interpolation

This allows you to control the smoothness of animations created with keyframes. Keyframe interpolation determines the change of values between keyframes.

Step 1

First, apply keyframes to the desired properties of a clip. You can do this by selecting the clip in the timeline and opening the Effects Control panel.

Step 2

Next, right-click on a keyframe in the Effects Control panel or the clip in the timeline. When you see the context menu, choose "Temporal Interpolation" to access the keyframe interpolation options.

Step 3

In the temporal Interpolation submenu, choose either Linear, Bezier, Auto Bezier, Ease-in, Ease-out, etc.

Step 4

Next, choose an interpolation method from the submenu to apply to the desired keyframes.

Applying the Auto Reframe Effect

The Auto Reframe effect in Adobe Premiere Pro allows you to automatically reframe and resize your videos for different aspect ratios and orientations.

Step 1

Import your clip.

Step 2

Drag the clip from the Project panel and drop it onto the timeline to add it to your sequence.

Step 3

Locate the clip in the timeline and select it. In the Effects panel, search for "Auto Reframe" or navigate to Video Effects > Transform > Auto Reframe. Click and drag the Auto Reframe effect onto the selected clip in the timeline.

Combining a Drop Shadow with Motion Effects

Follow the simple steps in the next paragraph to learn how to combine a drop shadow with motion effects.

Step 1

Import your footage.

Step 2

Create a new sequence by right clicking the footage in the project panel and selecting "New Sequence From Clip" to create a new sequence based on the clip's settings.

Step 3

In the Effects panel, search for the "Motion" effect and drag it onto your footage in the timeline.

Step 4

You can modify the parameters of the Motion effect to create the desired motion by going to the Effects panel.

Step 5

Go to the Effects panel, search for the "Drop Shadow" effect, and drag it onto your footage in the timeline.

Chapter 10: EDITING AND MIXING AUDIO

It is one thing to edit your audio; it is another thing to mix the audio well into the video. This chapter will explore what you need to know about editing and combining your audio clips. Whether you want to know how to set up an interface for your audio or adjust audio volume, this chapter got you covered.

Starting The Lesson

In this lesson, we will first examine how to set up the interface to work with audio. If the interface isn't set right, nothing else will work effectively. Read on.

Setting up The Interface to work With Audio

Setting up the interface involves creating an audio track, assigning an audio track, customizing the audio workspace, etc. Let's approach the subject matter in a step-by-step format.

Step 1

Launch Adobe Premiere Pro and create a new project.

Step 2

Go to the project panel and choose "Import" to import your audio files into the project.

Step 3

Proceed to the timeline panel, and choose "Add Tracks." In the pop-up dialog box, select the number of audio tracks you need. Click OK to create the tracks.

Step 4

Next, drag the imported audio files from the Project panel to the appropriate audio tracks in the Timeline panel. You can arrange them in chronological order or as desired.

Step 5

Adobe Premiere Pro offers dedicated workspaces optimized for audio editing. To switch to an audio-focused workspace, go to Window > Workspaces and select "Audio."

Examining Audio Characteristics

There are several audio tools provided by Adobe Premiere Pro that allows you to examine audio characteristics. Some of them are mentioned below.

- Audio meters
- Audio waveform display
- Audio effects rack
- Sound panel
- Audio channel mapping
- Audio track mixer
- Spectral frequency display

Adding Adobe Stock Audio

Here is how to add Adobe Stock Audio to your projects in Adobe Premiere Pro.

Step 1

Start by launching Adobe Premiere Pro.

Step 2

Go to the Adobe Stock website (stock.adobe.com) in your web browser and log in with your Adobe ID. If you don't have an Adobe ID, you must create one.

Step 3

Using the search bar, search for the Audio you want to use in your project.

Step 4

Click on the "License" button to license the audio clip.

Step 5

Return to Adobe Premiere Pro after licensing the audio clip.

Step 6

Click on "File" in the menu bar and select "Import" -> "Media" or use the shortcut Ctrl+I (Windows)

Step 7

Go to the import dialog box and go to the downloaded Adobe Stock audio file. Choose it and click "Import."

Step 8

The audio clip will now appear in the Adobe Premiere Pro project panel.

Adjusting Audio Volume

While working on your projects, you can adjust the volume of your audio by following the simple steps below.

Step 1

Open the Adobe Premiere Pro project.

Step 2

Locate the audio clip or track you want to adjust in the timeline.

Step 3

Click on the timeline and select the audio clip.

Step 4

In the "Effect Controls" panel, which is typically found in the top-left corner of the screen, you will see a section labeled "Volume" or "Audio Gain." It contains controls for adjusting the audio volume.

Step 5

If you want to adjust the overall volume of your clip, change the value of the "Volume" or "Level" field.

Auto-duck Music Level

You can lower the music level when there is dialogue. Auto Ducking automatically adjusts the volume of one audio track based on the levels of another track.

Step 1

Start by opening your Adobe Premiere Pro project.

Step 2

Next, place the music track and the dialogue or other audio tracks on separate tracks in the timeline. Make sure the tracks are correctly aligned.

Step 3

Now choose the music track. This can be done by clicking on the timeline.

Step 4

Go to the Effects Control panel, and locate the "Auto Ducking" in the "Audio tab."

Step 5

Enable Auto Ducking by checking the box next to "Enable" or "Ducking."

Creating a Split Edit

A split edit, or L-cut or J-cut, can quickly be done in Adobe Premiere Pro. Here is how to do it.

Step 1

Open your project in Adobe Premiere Pro.

Step 2

Go to the timeline and locate the point where the split edit will be created.

Step 3

Now choose the video and audio clip that you want to split.

Step 4

position the play head at the desired split edit point. This will extend the video or audio clip.

Step 5

Please select the desired clip (video or audio) by clicking on it in the timeline. Activate the "Ripple Edit Tool" by pressing the E key.

Step 6

Click and drag the edge of the selected clip to extend or shorten it.

Chapter 11: IMPROVING AUDIO

You can improve the audio of your clips by utilizing various tools. Improving audio is essential if your video clip will come out looking well. In this chapter, we will look at how you can improve audio using the essential sound panel and adjusting dialogue audio.

Starting the Lesson

To start this lesson, we will look at the essential sound panel and how it can be used to improve sound. The Essential Sound panel in Adobe Premiere Pro is a powerful tool that helps streamline and simplify audio editing. It provides a user-friendly interface with presets and intuitive controls for improving and fine-tuning the audio in your project.

109

Improving Audio with the Essential Sound Panel

Using the essential sound panel, you can improve the quality of your audio. You can add various effects to your audio using the essential sound panel.

Step 1

Open your project.

Step 2

Select the "Essential panel" by going to the Window menu.

Step 3

In the Essential Sound panel, you'll find various tabs representing different audio types and categories, such as Dialogue, Music, SFX, and Ambience. Click on the tab corresponding to the audio you want to work on.

Step 4

Go to the timeline and select the audio clip you want to enhance.

Step 5

There is a wide range of enhancements that can be done in the essential sound panel.

Step 4

Identify the type of audio you want to improve, such as dialogue or music, and click on the corresponding category.

Adjusting Dialogue Audio

Now that we have seen how to improve audio using an essential sound panel let us look at how to adjust dialogue audio in a few steps.

Step 1

Begin by importing your footage.

Step 2

Remember that if your dialogue audio is recorded separately from the video, you must sync them. Premiere Pro provides various methods to sync audio and video, such as using timecode or syncing based on audio waveforms.

Step 3

Now go ahead to select the dialogue clip in the timeline.

Step 4

Go to the "Window" menu and select "Essential Sound" to open the Essential Sound Panel.

Step 5

Assign the dialogue clip to the "Dialogue" category by selecting it from the drop-down menu.

Step 6

Using the "repair" option in the essential sound panel, you can reduce the background noise and enhance clarity.

Step 7

Use the "Volume" slider to set the overall volume level of the dialogue clip.

Chapter 12: ADDING VISUAL EFFECTS

Adding visual effects to your Adobe Premiere Pro can significantly improve the overall outlook of your project. Just as improving audio is done using the effects panel, adding visual effects is also achieved through the effects panel.

Starting the Lesson

The first thing that you will learn in this lesson is knowing how to work with visual effects. After that, we will show you how to apply master clip effects and mask your visual effects. All these will be shown to you using simple steps

Working with Visual Effects

Working with visual effects in Adobe Premiere Pro allows you to enhance the visual quality of your videos and add creative elements.

Step 1

Import your footage.

Step 2

Right-click on the imported footage and select "New Sequence from Clip." Choose the sequence settings depending on the requirements of your project.

Step 3

Open the effects panel.

Step 4

Browse through the effects and choose one.

Step 5

To apply a visual effect, drag and drop it onto a clip in the timeline. You can also select the clip and double-click on the effect in the Effects panel to apply it.

Masking and tracking visual effects

There are various tools provided by Adobe Premiere Pro for masking and tracking visual effects. This allows you to isolate areas of a frame and the movement of an object.

Step 1

Import your footage.

Step 2

Create a new sequence.

Step 3

Drag the video clip from the Project panel to the timeline. Select the clip on the timeline and navigate to the Effects Control panel.

Step 4

Navigate to the Effects panel. Search the "Opacity" section. Look for the square icon with a curved line called the Pen tool. Click on it to activate the Pen tool for creating masks.

Step 5

Now that the pen tool is selected, click on the clip in the Program Monitor to create a mask.

Step 6

The shape of the mask can be adjusted using the selection tool.

Step 8

To track the movement of an object within the frame, go to the Effects Control panel and click on the "Motion" or "Motion Tracking" option, depending on the version of Premiere Pro. Choose the "Track Motion" or "Track Selected Mask" option. Look out for the window that will appear.

Step 9

Start the tracking by clicking on the Play button.

Keyframing Effects

Keyframes can be used to animate and control the effects applied to your video clips. Keyframes let you set specific parameter values at different points in time, creating smooth transitions and animations.

Step 1

You want to start by applying the effect you want to animate to a video clip on the timeline. This can be done by dragging the effect from the Effects panel onto the clip.

Step 2

Locate the effect parameter you want to animate in the Effects Control panel.

Step 3

Next, move the play head on the timeline to the desired starting point for your animation. Adjust the effect parameter value to the desired setting for that point in time. A keyframe will automatically be created.

Step 4

Set additional keyframes by moving the play head to another point where you want to change the effect parameter value.

Step 5

If you wish to modify the values of existing keyframes, then select the keyframe(s) on the timeline or in the Effect Controls panel and adjust the effect parameter value in the Effects Control panel.

Using Effect Presets

It's essential you understand what effects presets are in Adobe Premiere Pro. Effects presets are preconfigured settings that allow you to quickly apply a specific look or effect to your video clips.

Step 1

Begin by importing your footage.

Step 2

Apply an effect on the clip using the effects panel.

Step 3

Now that the clip is selected go to the Effects Control panel. This panel displays the effect settings and controls for the selected clip.

Step 4

In the Effects panel, you'll find a variety of folders containing different types of effects. Browse these folders to see the effect you want to apply, such as color correction, transitions, or stylization.

Step 5

Once you've found the effect you want to use, double-click on it to apply it to the selected footage in the timeline.

Step 6

To use effect presets, click the "Presets" dropdown menu in the Effect Controls panel.

Exploring Frequently Used Effects

Here are some of the frequently used effects in Adobe Premiere Pro.

- **Ultra Key**

This effect is used for green screen or chroma keying. It helps you remove a specific color from the footage, such as a green background, and replace it with another image or video.

- **Opacity**

This effect controls the transparency of your footage. You can use it to create fade-ins and fade-outs or blend multiple clips.

- **Gaussian Blur**

The Gaussian Blur effect allows you to blur specific parts of your footage. It can be used for various purposes, such as blurring faces for privacy or creating depth-of-field effects.

Using the Render and Replace command

This helpful feature allows you to replace a clip in your timeline with a rendered version. This can help improve playback performance, especially with high-resolution or effects-heavy footage.

Step 1

Load your project after firing up Adobe Premiere Pro.

Step 2

Go to the project panel and locate the clip you want to render and replace in the timeline.

Step 3

Right-click on the clip and select "Render and Replace" from the context menu.

Step 4

Notice that a new dialog box will appear, which allows you to customize the settings for the rendered clip.

Step 5

Click OK after you've set the desired parameters. Premiere Pro will start rendering the selected clip based on your specified settings.

Step 6

After the rendering process, Premiere Pro will automatically replace the original clip in your timeline with the rendered version.

Chapter 13: APPLYING COLOR CORRECTION AND GRADING

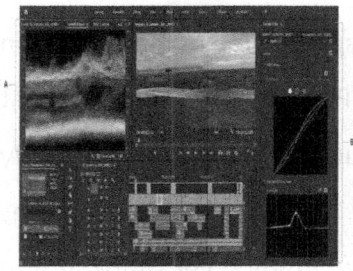

Applying color correction and grading in Adobe Premiere Pro is all about manipulating the colors and general look of your video footage to achieve a desired aesthetic or fix any issues with the original footage. In this chapter, we will look at how to use colors and grading in Adobe Premiere Pro.

Starting the Lesson

The first lesson we will look at in this chapter is understanding display color management. Display color management in Adobe Premiere Pro refers to ensuring that the colors in your video appear accurately and consistently across different devices and viewing environments. Let's look at it in more detail in the next paragraph.

Understanding Display Color Management

Display color management involves managing the color space of your footage, calibrating your monitor, and configuring the color settings in Premiere Pro to maintain color accuracy throughout your editing workflow. Some of the essentials that you should know about understanding color management are:

- Monitor Calibration
- Color Spaces
- Project Settings
- Viewing LUTs
- Export Settings

Following the Color Adjustment Workflow

The color adjustment workflow in Adobe Premiere Pro is a series of steps to improve and fine-tune the colors of your video footage.

Step 1

Start by importing your footage.

Step 2

Create a new sequence.

Step 3

Next, search for the "Lumetri Color" effect and drag it onto the footage on the timeline. This effect provides a wide range of controls for color correction.

Step 4

Now use the additional controls in the "Lumetri Color" effects to better the look of your footage.

Using Comparison View

The comparison view helps you to compare two different frames side by side. This makes it easier to analyze and match the visual elements.

Step 1

Begin by opening the comparison view.

Step 2

From the Settings menu, select "Comparison View" to enable it.

Step 3

Go to the program monitor, and you will see a split-screen layout. The left side represents the current frame or clip, while the right is the comparison source.

Step 4

In the Settings menu, you have several options to customize the comparison view. You can choose to compare different frames, clips, or sequences.

Step 5

You can make adjustments with the comparison view enabled.

Matching Colors

When the colors of multiple clips are adjusted, and a consistent look is created, then the process of matching colors in Adobe Premiere Pro has been achieved.

Step 1

Import your clips and create a new sequence.

Step 2

Apply some color correction to the central clip.

Step 3

Right-click on the primary clip with the Lumetri Color effect applied and select "Copy" from the context menu.

Step 4

Next, select the secondary clip that you want to match to the primary clip. Right-click on the selected clip(s) and choose "Paste Attributes" from the context menu. In the Paste Attributes dialog box, ensure that the "Lumetri Color" option is selected, and click "OK." This will apply the same Lumetri Color settings from the primary and secondary clips (s).

Step 5

You may need to fine-tune further the color adjustments to match the visuals precisely. Select each secondary clip individually, go to the Lumetri Color controls, and make any necessary adjustments to achieve a seamless color match.

Exploring the Color-adjustment Effects

Here are some widespread color adjustment effects available in Adobe Premiere Pro.

- **Lumetri Color**

The Lumetri Color effect is a powerful tool that provides comprehensive color correction and grading capabilities. It offers various controls to adjust exposure, contrast, saturation, vibrance, shadows, highlights, and more.

- **RGB Curves**

This effect helps you adjust the red, blue, and green channels of your footage. Curves are provided for each channel which allows you to manipulate the tonal range.

Other color adjustment effects you can use in Adobe Premiere Pro are:

- Color Balance
- Three-way color corrector
- Color wheels
- Vibrance

Correcting Color Offset

The RGB Curves effect can correct color offset in Adobe Premiere Pro. Follow the steps below.

Step 1

Select the clip you want to adjust on the timeline.

Step 2

Search for "RGB Curves" in the Effects panel.

Step 3

Drag the RGB Curves effect onto the selected clip.

Step 4

To correct the color offset, locate the channel causing the offset.

Using Special Color Effects

Adobe Premiere Pro offers a range of special color effects that you can apply to your footage to achieve unique and creative looks. These effects can help enhance your project's visual style or create specific moods. Below are some special color effects you can use in Adobe Premiere Pro.

- **Vignette**

This allows users to darken or lighten the edges of their footage, creating a spotlight or framing effect. It can help draw attention to the center of the frame or add a vintage look to your footage.

- **Tint**

The Tint effect lets you add a specific color tint to your footage. You can use it to give your footage a nostalgic or vintage look or to create a stylized effect by adding a particular cast of color.

Creating a Distinctive Look

How can one create a distinctive look in Adobe Premiere Pro? It is simply by applying various color grading techniques, effects, and adjustments to your footage to achieve a unique and visually appealing style.

Step 1

Before diving into the technical aspects, envision the style or mood you want to create for your footage.

Step 2

Start with color correction. This can be done by using the "Lumetri Color" effect.

Step 3

Once the basic corrections are in place, apply color grading techniques to create the desired look.

Step 4

Experiment with Vignettes, Black, and White, to further create your distinctive look.

Chapter 14: EXPLORING COMPOSITING TECHNIQUES

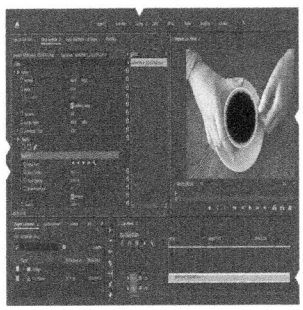

This chapter is about compositing techniques and their application to your projects. Compositing in Adobe Premiere Pro involves combining multiple visual elements, such as images, videos, and graphics, to create a unified composition.

Starting the Lesson

We will begin this lesson by looking at what an alpha channel is. If you have been using editing apps for a while, you may have encountered the term "Alpha Channel." For those that haven't, you are in luck because we will tell you what an Alpha channel is in the next paragraph.

What is an Alpha Channel?

An Alpha channel refers to an additional channel of information that is used to define the transparency or opacity of a video clip or image. An Alpha Channel contains grayscale data, where white represents full opacity (completely visible), and black represents full transparency (completely invisible). The shades of gray in between represent varying levels of transparency. When a video or image contains an Alpha Channel, it allows for non-rectangular or irregularly shaped elements to be composited together seamlessly.

Making Compositing Part of Your Project

Below is how to make compositing part of your project in Adobe Premiere Pro.

Step 1

Import your footage.

Step 2

Next, create a new sequence.

Step 3

Arrange your clips by dragging and dropping them on the timeline.

Step 4

To fine-tune the composite, you can adjust the opacity of your clips by selecting them on the timeline and adjusting the Opacity slider in the Effect Controls panel.

Adjusting Alpha Channel Transparencies

The below steps will show you how you can adjust the transparency of your Alpha Channel.

Step 1

After Importing your footage, creating the new sequence, and adding them to the timeline, Select the clip on the timeline and navigate to the Effect Controls panel. Look for the Opacity property and adjust the slider to modify the overall transparency of the clip. A value of 100% means the clip is fully opaque, while a value of 0% means the clip is fully transparent.

Color Keying a Green Screen Shot

Color keying is also known as chroma keying. To achieve a color key on your green screenshot, carefully follow these steps.

Step 1

Import your footage. Next, create a new sequence and place the footage on your timeline.

Step 2

Select the greenscreen footage on the timeline, then go to the Effects panel and search for "Ultra Key." Drag the Ultra Key effect onto the greenscreen footage.

Step 3

Go to the Effects panel, and you will find the Ultra Key effect settings. Use the eyedropper tool under the Key Color option to sample the green color from the greenscreen footage. The Ultra Key effect will automatically key out the selected color, making it transparent.

Partially Masking Clips

The in-built masking tools can easily mask clips in Adobe Premiere Pro.

Step 1

After Importing your footage, create a sequence and add the footage to your timeline.

Step 2

Select the clip on the timeline and navigate to the Effect Controls panel. Look for the Opacity property and click on the small triangle to expand the options.

Step 3

Look for a pen tool in the opacity property section. Click on the Pen tool, and the mask creation mode will be active.

Step 4

With the Pen tool active, click and drag on the clip to create a shape that defines the area you want to mask.

Chapter 15: CREATING NEW GRAPHICS

It is important to note that Adobe Premiere Pro is primarily video editing software. However, it offers some basic graphic creation capabilities. We are going to explore some of that in this chapter.

Starting The Lesson

The lesson begins with a quick tour of the essential graphics panel. It is a robust tool that allows you to create, customize, and manage graphics and motion graphics directly within the application. It gives a user-friendly interface for designing and animating graphics, making it easier to create professional-looking titles. Let's talk about it in more detail.

Exploring The Essential Graphics Panel

To explore the essential graphics panel, you must first know how to open it. To open the Essential Graphics panel, go to the top menu bar and select "Window" > "Essential Graphics." Alternatively, you can choose the Graphics workspace, which automatically opens the Essential Graphics panel and other related panels. It also allows you to work with graphic templates, which are pre-designed graphics that can be customized and reused in different projects. You can access a range of built-in templates, import external templates, or create templates to streamline your workflow.

Mastering Video Typography Essentials

To master video typography essentials, one must master the fundamentals of typography and utilize the tools provided by Adobe Premiere Pro effectively. Some of the essentials of Video typography include working with text in Adobe Premiere, Applying Typography techniques, Fine-tuning, and exporting.

Creating New Titles

The process of creating new titles in Adobe Premiere Pro is a pretty simple one. The following paragraph explains it in a step-by-step guide.

Step 1

Open your project.

Step 2

Next, go to the "Graphics" workspace by selecting Window > Workspaces > Graphics. In the "Graphics" workspace, click on the "Browse" tab to access the "Essential Graphics" panel.

Step 3

Click on the "Browse" tab to access the "Essential Graphics" panel in the "Graphics Workspace."

Step 4

To create a title from scratch, click on the "New Item" button at the bottom of the "Essential Graphics" panel and select "Title" from the drop-down menu. This will create a new blank title.

Text Styles

There are various text styles that you can apply to your projects in Adobe Premiere Pro. Below are some of the common ones.

- Bold and Italic
- Underline and strikethrough
- All caps
- Small caps
- Shadow, etc.

Working With Shapes and Logos

When working with shapes and logos, you can add graphic elements, create overlays, and enhance the visual appeal of your video projects.

Step 1

Open your project and navigate to the "Graphics" workspace by selecting Window > Workspaces > Graphics.

Step 2

Click the "Browse" tab in the "Essential Graphics" panel.

Step 3

Locate the shape or logo that you wish to import.

Step 4

Drag and drop the file into the "Essential Graphics" panel or use the "Import Motion Graphics Template" button at the bottom to import the file.

Making a Title Roll

A title roll effect makes the text moves vertically from top to bottom or vice versa.

Step 1

Start by creating a new title.

Step 2

Now customize the title text.

Step 3

In the "Edit" tab, go to the "Transform" section and change the "Position" values to move the title to the desired starting position on the screen.

Step 4

With the title still selected, go to the beginning of the timeline where you want to roll to. Click the stopwatch icon next to the "Position" property in the "Edit" tab to set the initial keyframe.

Step 5

Move to the end of the timeline where you want the roll to end. Change the "Position" values to move the title to the desired ending position.

Working with Motion Graphics Templates

This lets you leverage pre-designed graphics elements, including titles, lower thirds, transitions, and animations, to enhance your video projects. To access your motion graphics template, Select the "Graphics" workspace by selecting Window > Workspaces > Graphics. Click the "Browse" tab in the "Essential Graphics" panel. The

"Browse" tab displays a collection of pre-built Motion Graphics templates that you can use.

Adding Captions

Adding captions is handy when relaying an essential message to your audience. It allows you to include text corresponding to the spoken dialogue or narration.

Step 1

Import your video footage into Adobe Premiere Pro by creating a new project and dragging your video files into the Project panel.

Step 2

Next, create a new caption track by clicking the "New Item" button in the Project panel and selecting "Captions."

Step 3

Choose the caption track you created and go to "Essentials Graphics Panel."

Step 4

In the Essential Graphics panel, click on the "Browse" button next to the "Text" field and select "Open Text."

Step 5

A text box will appear on your video preview screen. Type in the captions for the corresponding timecode in the text box.

Chapter 16: EXPORTING FRAMES, CLIPS, AND SEQUENCES

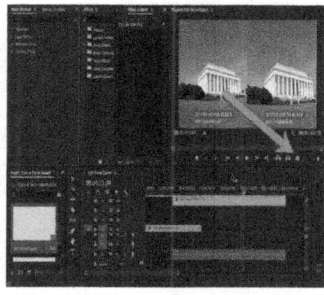

When you are done working on your clips and sequences, then comes the part where you need to export it. Exporting is usually a straightforward process. So, you should not have a problem grasping this chapter.

Starting The Lesson

We set the ball rolling by looking at how to make quick export using Adobe Premiere

Pro. Quick exports can be done using even keyboard shortcuts. The purpose of quick exports is to save you time as you work. So, how is it done? Check the next paragraph.

Making Quick Exports

The steps below show you how to make quick exports using Adobe Premiere Pro.

Step 1

Select the sequence or the timeline portion you want to export.

Step 2

Once the desired sequence is chosen, go to "File" > "Export" > "Media" or use the shortcut Ctrl+M (Windows) or Command+M (Mac).

Step 3

Choose the format and other settings for export. After setting up the export settings, you can choose the output destination by clicking on the "Output Name" field and specifying a file name and location for the exported file. Click on "Export" when you are done.

Understanding The Full Media Export Options

Adobe Premiere Pro provides several media export options for different formats, resolutions, codecs, and platforms. Here are the main export options available in Adobe Premiere Pro:

- MOV
- MP4

- AVI
- WMV

Output Name and Destination: This helps specify the name and location where you want to save the exported media file. You can also export directly to an external drive or a specific folder.

Export Queue: Instead of exporting immediately, you can add your export job to the queue. This allows you to continue working on other projects while Premiere Pro processes the export in the background. You can access the Export Queue from the top-right corner of the Export Settings window.

Exporting Single Frames

Using the Export Frame function, you can export single frames from your project. This allows you to capture a specific frame as an image file.

Step 1

Navigate to the frame you want to export in the Timeline or Program Monitor. Use the playhead or the navigation controls to locate the desired frame accurately.

Step 2

When at the desired frame, go to the Program Monitor panel and find the camera icon in the bottom right corner. It is called the Export Frame button.

Step 3

Click on the Export Frame button to open the Export Frame dialog box.

Step 4

After selecting the desired options, click the OK button to export the frame.

Exporting a Master File

Here is how you can export a master file in Adobe Premiere Pro.

Step 1

Start by opening your project in Adobe Premiere Pro.

Step 2

Go to File > Export > Media to open the Export Settings window.

Step 3

In the Export Settings window, choose the desired format for your master file. It is advisable to select a high-quality and lossless format for a master file.

Step 4

Customize the settings for the chosen format. You can adjust parameters like resolution, frame rate, bit depth, codec options, audio settings, and more.

Step 5

Specify the destination and output name and click on the export button.

Working With Adobe Media Encoder

The Media Encoder of Adobe is a great software that works in tandem with Adobe Media Media Pro. It allows you to process and export your media files using various formats, codecs, and presets.

To work with Adobe Media Encoder, set up your export settings in Premiere Pro: In Adobe Premiere Pro, go to File > Export > Media to open the Export Settings window. Next, send your sequence or media to Adobe Media Encoder for processing. To open Adobe Media Encoder, click the "Queue" button in the Export Settings window. In Adobe Media Encoder, your export job will appear in the Queue panel. Here, you can further customize the export settings if needed. You can adjust the output format, codec, resolution, bitrate, audio settings, etc.

Uploading to Social Media

There are built-in features provided by Adobe Premiere Pro that can simplify uploading your videos directly to social media platforms.

Step 1

Make sure your video is fully edited and ready for upload. Trim, add effects, adjust audio, and make any necessary adjustments in your sequence.

Step 2

Go to File > Export > Media in Adobe Premiere Pro to open the Export Settings window.

Step 3

Next, select the desired format for uploading to social media platforms.

Step 4

Specify the name and location where you want to save the exported video file.

Choose a location that is easily accessible. Export the video when you are ready.

Exchanging Projects with Other Editing Applications

Through standard interchange formats, Adobe Premiere Pro allows for the exchange of projects. Below are some standard interchange formats to exchange projects between Adobe Premiere Pro and other applications.

XML is a widely used interchange format that transfers project data between different editing applications.

AAF is another interchange format that supports the exchange of project data between different editing applications. Premiere Pro can export projects as AAF files by going to File > Export > AAF. AAF files can be imported into various editing software, including Avid Media Composer and DaVinci Resolve.

Chapter 17: Advance Functions

Adobe Premiere Pro offers several advanced functions to enhance your editing workflow. Let's look at a few of them.

- **Collaboration and versioning**

Using Adobe Team Projects, multiple editors can collaborate on the same project simultaneously. Team Projects allows for real-time updates, version control, and project management, making it easier to work with a team on a shared project.

- **Proxy workflow**

If you are working with high-resolution or resource-intensive footage, be rest assured that Adobe Premiere Pro allows you to create proxy files for smoother editing performance. Proxy files are lower-resolution versions of your media that maintain the same timecode and metadata.

Troubleshooting Adobe Premiere Pro

If you encounter issues or need to troubleshoot problems in Adobe Premiere Pro, here are some standard troubleshooting steps you can follow:

- **Update**

This is the most common approach for troubleshooting Adobe Premiere Pro. Check for updates in the Creative Cloud desktop application and install any available updates. Newer versions often include bug fixes and performance improvements.

- **Check for System Requirements**

You need to ensure that your system requirements can run Adobe Premiere Pro. Also, ensure that your graphics card drivers are up to date.

FAQs

- **Which operating systems are supported by Adobe Premiere Pro?**

Adobe Premiere Pro is available for both Windows and macOS operating systems.

- **How much does Adobe Premiere Pro cost?**

Adobe Premiere Pro is available through Adobe Creative Cloud subscription plans. The pricing can vary depending on the subscription type (individual, business, student, etc.) and the duration of the subscription.

171

Conclusion

This Adobe Premiere Pro eBook is a comprehensive guide on mastering the powerful video editing software that is Adobe Premiere Pro. It provides comprehensive guidance on video editing, from essential functions to advanced techniques, allowing users to unleash their creativity and produce professional-grade videos. Using step-by-step instructions, this guide empowers readers to navigate the software's features confidently and efficiently. With Adobe Premiere Pro's constant updates and evolving capabilities, we are confident that users now have the knowledge and skills needed to stay ahead in the rapidly changing world of video editing.

Made in United States
North Haven, CT
07 November 2023

43723297R00095